The Old and The New

Karen Turnbull

BookLeaf Publishing

India | USA | UK

Presentation by *BookLeaf Publishing*

Web: www.bookleafpub.com

E-mail: info@bookleafpub.com

ISBN: 9789357445870

First edition 2022

DEDICATION

To Rob:

without whom there wouldn't be any poetry.

PREFACE

I have written a lot of poetry. Most of it has been pretty awful and a lot dependant on my age or state of mind. But some poems have become treasures in my heart - they are the "old" poems in this book.
And the new? only time will tell if they become treasure, or dust.

Unrequited

Woken up
Like an enemy within
The desire to love
and be loved…
With nowhere to go.

It paces the floor of my heart
Causing injury and misery.

It shouldn't be this way!
Heart fire,
Burning me to ashes,
Go back to sleep!

I don't need you
Don't want you,
you just cause pain,
Beating me black and blue

Changing my world from bright
To grey, go away!

Go away.

Winter Storms

Here comes the winter wind
Shoving its way through.
The bully boy who knocks
down trees
Driving water into places
It would not normally go.
Where is your sweet cousin
That dances a polka
with the leaves
And lets poppy heads
sway to and fro?

Roll on sunshine and
gentle warm air,
Fluffy white clouds and the
rainbow May fair.

Draw near fields of blue linseed,
Burnished bronze
in the summer sun;
And bring forth a new creed
Where winter is for ever done.

Lime Green

There is no way to explain
The terrible void
And lonely path,
This burning desire.
How can I say
About the everyday dull ache,
The sudden breathless pain
Caused by a baby grow in a shop.
What words to use
For the wrenching grief
The earth shifting sense of loss
For the children I have never had.
And who is there to tell?
How could my friends
With their child filled lives
Ever understand?
And even those who
have suffered
The Good Friday
of childlessness
Now have their
parental Easter day.
And what can I say to a church
That helps people understand
gods love

Through the feelings they have
for their children?
Who is there then,
That knows this pain
Or who would at least
cry with me,
Rather than giving
fluffy platitudes
Of oh there's time yet
Or so and so has children…
These words
They comfort only the giver.
They leave me bereft
Still barren
Still childless.

Churchyard

I love the churchyard.
Many find it a place of fear,
Where TV nightmares come to life.

But it's a different place to me,
As I walk through,
on route to elsewhere.

I hear the rustle of
real angel wings
As they guard the gateways
Letting the stone angels
sleep on.

It's a place where the best
fairy tale
Sort of magic is found
With apple blossom
snowing down

And birdsong in

dapple sun drenched air.

Even in the night I see beauty
On the moonlit graves
Of the sleeping saved,

Waiting for the last alleluia
When those gateway sentinels
Of the graveyard

Will have finished
their service of love.

God Goggles

I am empty.

You are full.

I have two left feet,
one of which is in my mouth;

You danced at the dawn of time
And have the words
of eternal life.

Yet here I am, set in this life.So, I ask that you
would
fill my empty hands,

Untie my tongue and
teach me how to dance.

I am blind.

You are all seeing.

My mind is dim.
You know all things.

So, I ask that you
would give me

God goggles

So I can see through your eyes
And hold your wisdom
in my heart.

Then I can be
your hands and feet,
And give the wisdom and love
You put in my hands to others.

Star

A star you are.
Shining bright in his hand.
You may feel

Like you are
Oh so much dirt
Only good underfoot
But you're not.

Loved you are
By His eternal heart.
You may feel

Like you are not worth
The time of day.
But you are.

Open up the door
Let yourself be loved

Shine as you should
Because He never
Makes mistakes

Even if we do.

The Astronomer's Prayer

Jesus you are
The Polaris of my life
Whether I'm having a
Big Bear of a problem
Or just a Minor
Irritation.
You never shift.
Your light remains true
As everything else revolves
Around you.
Spring summer
Autumn winter
Whatever position
My life is in,
You are my Polaris

Body

Bringer of
tempest,

barometer

of the
heart

Morse code
of five senses

translator

for my
mind

fragile vessel

the sweet
ship

in which my soul

navigates

this
world.

Alchemy

There are days where
the brightest sun
cannot penetrate
the grey of sorrow

When all the world
doesn't seem enough
to outweigh
this heavy load

Yet your presence
the knowledge
of your unfailing love
still provides

Alchemy for my heart.

Mentor

I used to go
and clean
her brass ornaments.

She paid me
each week
with money

And wisdom

That was later
to save my life.

Ruach, Breath of Heaven

A million blessings
you shower upon us
like dandelion seeds
gently floating down.
But we who only see
the mire and the mud
forget to be with upward gaze
filled with hope.
A quiet breath
of Holy presence
we so often miss
in the utter roar
of our hearts desires
when only a moment of stillness
would usher in heaven to our hearts.

Before

A year and a half ago
we had never heard
of drive through test centres
never seen
masks in the streets and shops.
Before
one hundred and thirty-five thousand
British people died
the only danger from football crowds
was beer and aggression.
But no horse and rider
can stop the invisible killer
from silently passing from fan to fan
and even though as the double vaccinated
we have the grace of lesser illness
our lives have changed forever.

Homeless

Covid has scattered the flock
we have forgotten how to gather
and restrictions mean
there is no immediate route home.
We reside on the temporary sofa
of another church.
In all this Lord,
what does it look like
to come together as your people
to worship and serve and learn?
How do we remain faithful to you
and kind to others?
I long for us to go together,
But we are still forced apart.
Come Holy Spirit
guide us by your light.
Come Lord Jesus
and shepherd us home.

Centring

Night comes.
the dark curls around,
like a soft blanket,
stars visible
through the skylight.
I light a candle
for comfort,
and the day drops away
as my soul
finds you.

The Hours

Vigil:
In the quiet night hour
Hidden grace starts to germinate
Morning frost awakens

Prime:
Community gathers
First coffee and open hearts
Morning sun blesses

Compline:
All return home to
Gather the weight of the day
A final offering

Meds

Hello little white pill
you who stop my mind
from folding in on itself
until the thought of
choosing which socks to put on
is impossible.
I'm glad I have you, and my life
but you signify all the stigma
the knowledge that
my illness is acceptable
until I display symptoms.
So i need you
not only to stay well
but to give me the time
for the long slow heal
without the added pressure
of unacceptability.
You are my
anti - social isolation
pill.
Except when you are not strong enough
to hold back the tide.
And then I have to drown a while
alone.

Delay the everyday

Burnt out brain
the cinders of my mind
blown all around
by the slightest task.
I need time away
to regroup
to delay everyday life
in favour of
the internal work of rebirth
A phoenix rising from the ashes
of bad choices and injured soul.
To take a better balanced path
the light of your wisdom
leading the way.

Crack the concrete

Grey cemented life
I am a country born foreigner
living in the middle of the city.
Your hard streets
and harsh light
assault of noise
and crush of humanity,
Would wash me away
if i were not able
to pass through
the back door veil
into the garden sanctuary.
even though city life asserts itself
the gentle hum of bumblebees
and warm afternoon light
soak into my soul
as I am cocooned in green all around.

Spider season

Fat bottomed spiders
are swinging
all over my garden.
Their brazen webs
stretch across
paths and pots and back door.
I imagine tiny shaking fists
as I put them to one side.
Temporarily disrupted
they re-weave their gossamer kingdom
miniature palaces
sparking in the morning dew.

Sonnnetish

In the depths of the velveteen night sky
Long burning lights tell their ancient story
I'm drawn close to you, let my soul fly
The quiet, the moonlight, whisper your glories.

Then all around the ripe golden harvest
Is shouting out your faithful provision
While autumn leaves, as trees begin to rest,
call me to a deeper contemplation.

The more I allow myself to notice now
The greater my experience of eternity.
Seasons and the smallest of things are how
You draw me into your perfect triunity.

All that's known of you, there's always more
May your loving kindness be, my perfect law.

Haiku

Creativity
Life blood of my inner world
A new day for words.